What Happened When He Went to the Store for Bread

POEMS BY

ALDEN NOWLAN

What Happened When He Went to the Store for Bread

POEMS BY
ALDEN NOWLAN

Chosen and Introduced by Thomas R. Smith

Foreword by Robert Bly

NINETIES PRESS
SAINT PAUL, MINNESOTA

The editor would like to thank especially Robert Bly, Allan Cooper, Robert Gibbs, Michael Kincaid, and Claudine Nowlan for their gracious assistance and support at crucial stages in the preparation of What Happened When He Went to the Store for Bread.

Frontispiece photo from the collection of Claudine Nowlan (photographer unknown).

Cover painting, "Sign and Harrier," by Alex Colville, 1970. Reproduced by permission of Musée National d'Art Moderne, Centre Georges Pompidou, Paris.

First Edition

Designed by Cats Pajamas, Inc.
Printed in the United States of America by Thomson-Shore, Inc.
No government funds were used in the production of this book.

Library of Congress Cataloging-in-Publication Data

Nowlan, Alden.
What happened when he went to the store for bread : poems / by Alden Nowlan ; chosen and introduced by Thomas R. Smith ; foreword by Robert Bly. — 1st ed.
p. cm.
Includes bibliographical references.
ISBN 1-883070-00-7 : 10.00
I. Title
PR9199.3.N6W43 1993
811'.54—dc20 93-14682
CIP

Published by
NINETIES PRESS
Saint Paul, Minnesota

Distributed by
Ally Press Center
524 Orleans Street
Saint Paul, Minnesota 55107

Contents

Glance Down at Things That Have Fallen

Meeting the Eye of Anybody

Foreword

This Moment of Suffering and Confusion

IT IS A PLEASURE to welcome the first large selection from the whole range of Alden Nowlan's work to readers south of Canada. He belongs to the brave ones, those who can talk of terrible things, and in his art, still remember that we are listening. Like Kafka, he can look at ordinary events with the eyes of the unprivileged.

One night as he walks out of his newspaper office, he sees a young American sailor yelling at a girl he has been with all evening who is drunk and kneeling on the sidewalk. Young men are privileged, capable of almost anything, when with Navy buddies. I remember it well. He doesn't know what to do about this woman, he doesn't know where she lives, the shore patrol could come–

> –and what keeps this from being squalid is
> what's happening to him inside . . .
> he's finding out what it means
> to be a man and how different it is
> from the way that only hours ago he imagined it.

A little like Stephen Crane, he learned to write as a newspaper reporter.

We could call him a teacher of grief. He doesn't pull us away into the sky, nor hint elegantly at what he wants to say and will later, but instead he wants everything in *this* poem. This moment of suffering and confusion is the real place where we touch our reason for being born. He doesn't recommend changing the subject; he says, as the writer, we had better go on with the poem, find a way through the resistant syntax, overcome our desire to stop now while we all still look good, go on searching for the phrase that will really make us feel small (as small as we really are)–compared to Michelangelo's

David—and by pushing ahead honor the greatness of language, the unspeakable gift of being able to participate at all in art and poetry, get it down, say it, and then be quiet.

He knows what very few writers know—how many people despise themselves. His eloquence does not flow from study of Roman speeches, nor from having observed sensitive people say the appropriate thing at the appropriate moment, though we all admire that, but he is eloquent because the curtain between him and his brutal fallen-man state is thin.

He writes tough poems as a parent. He knows how important the moment is when his son says, "I'll be fifteen tomorrow, can I have a whole bottle of beer?" The father watches himself hand his son a warm beer, because "there are only enough cool ones for the guests." "It doesn't matter," the son says. "It's okay." Nowlan later sees the beer bottle back in the refrigerator with only a few sips gone,

> . . . thinking
> of the petty treason
> we commit so often
> against those we love,
> the confidence games
> in which parents play
> their children for suckers.

He doesn't talk of the missing Grail, nor the paralysis the culture has gone through after the withering glance thrown by the Protestant myth-haters; he imagines no Paradises, nor the heavens where the irrational singers go in their sweetness, as Rumi does; he doesn't make magnificent cellos out of sound, as Marvell does. What does he do? He follows the soul as it walks down a corridor, and finds as Kafka sometimes did a horse-groom about to rape a hired girl, or a dog eating a kitten who is still alive. And, to paraphrase:

> . . . what keeps this from being squalid is
> what's happening to us inside . . .
> we're finding out what it means
> to be a human being and how different it is
> from the way that only hours ago we imagined it.

—Robert Bly

Introduction

In Praise of Alden Nowlan

ALDEN NOWLAN WAS BORN on January 25, 1933 in Hants County, Nova Scotia, a region so isolated that in the late Fifties Nowlan could say of it, "There are men here / who have never heard of Canada." His poem "Summer" weds vivid images to the sense of loneliness and desperation Nowlan experienced as a child of the Depression in that windy, thin-soiled coastal valley:

> It's summer yet but still the cold
> coils through these fields at dusk, the gray Atlantic
> haunting the hollows and a black bitch barking
> between a rockpile and a broken fence
> out on a hill a mile from town where maybe
> a she-bear, groggy with blueberries, listens
> and the colt, lonesome, runs in crooked circles.

Freeman Nowlan, a tenacious and unimaginative man, managed to subsist by doing seasonal work in the sawmill and woods. Nowlan says of him, "My father worked for more than 50 years and never, to my knowledge, had a permanent, year-round job in all that time, although God knows he was willing enough."[1] In "It's Good to Be Here," Nowlan envisions his unpromising origins without apparent exaggeration:

> I'm in trouble, she said
> to him. That was the first
> time in history that anyone
> had ever spoken of me.
>
> It was 1932 when she
> was just fourteen years old
> and men like him

worked all day for
one stinking dollar.

Raised by his Irish grandmothers, Nowlan found an escape in literature, teaching himself to read at age five. "I was Jack London reborn, achingly aware of my enormous ignorance, gluttonously devouring any scrap of knowledge, reading great stacks of books on almost any imaginable subject."[2] At 14, Nowlan had read, in addition to the entire contents of the small regional library in Windsor, the Bible cover to cover three times, not so much from religiosity as the fact that it was the single book his father tolerated in their house.

Almost as soon as he was able to read, Nowlan began to write poems and stories. What is most remarkable about these early literary efforts is that they were conducted in utmost secrecy, without evident support from family or community. In fact, Nowlan did not tell his father he wrote poetry until he left Windsor at the age of 19 to work as a reporter for the *Hartland Observer* in western New Brunswick. In rural Nova Scotia, as in so many other North American places of that time, literary interests were associated, if one happened to be male, with a shameful effeminacy. "Even today," he said in a 1983 interview, "if I'm working on a poem and someone enters the room—anyone—I automatically cover the paper with my hands."[3]

In one of his poems of this period, "Weakness," Nowlan says: "My father hates weakness worse than hail." Forcibly crushing such "weakness" invariably entailed throttling impulses for kindness, gentleness, and compassion toward other human beings. Nowlan's early poems reiterate a connection between cruelty and pride as acceptable public expressions; one may show kindness or affection only when safe from the threat of ridicule. In "Flossie at School" Nowlan secretively declares his liking for an awkward girl tormented by older boys:

And afterward I was ashamed
for crying when she cried.

Nowlan's formal education ended after a month in the fifth grade, roughly matching the length of his father's. The oppressive environment of Hants County offered Nowlan little reason to hope that he would not follow Freeman Nowlan into a life of brute poverty and labor. Driven to seek solitude within himself, Nowlan was widely believed at this time to be mildly retarded, an added humiliation which surely deepened his empathy for the outsiders and misfits for whom he so compassionately speaks in his poems and stories. One can imagine the agonizing frustration that led him to formulate, "The ultimate indignity is loneliness without privacy."[4]

Working in his teens as a pulp peeler, night watchman at a sawmill and road worker for the Nova Scotia Department of Highways, Nowlan managed at last to secure employment at the *Hartland Observer*, a province away, on the strength of a self-authored letter of reference. He writes of the chain of associations leading to his escape in the poem "What Happened When He Went to the Store for Bread" with wonderful feeling for the small events which carry the awesome weight of contingency or fate:

> What would I have been if I hadn't left there
> when I did? I would have almost certainly
> gone mad; I think I might have killed somebody.
> But even if something else had saved me
> from madness, I would not be the same person.
> I'd have spent thirty years in a different world
> and come to look at things in such a different way
> that even my memories of childhood and youth
> would be different; it might even seem to me now
> that there was never anything to escape from.

Nowlan arrived in Hartland, New Brunswick, in 1952, and soon began to publish his poems in literary magazines in Canada and the U.S. In 1958 the University of New Brunswick published his first chapbook of poems, *The Rose and the Puritan*. Two large collections of poetry and an autobiographical novel soon followed. The early poems range over locales in Nova Scotia and New Brunswick geographically and culturally so consistent as to appear identical. One hears in these poems echoes of Edgar Lee Masters and Edwin Arlington Robinson, not only for the complete, self-referential world they create, but in the basic conception of such character studies as "Warren Pryor" and "Andy Shaw," which capture in a few sturdily constructed metric lines some deep tension between the intent and actions of their protagonists.

Life in New Brunswick entailed its own hardships. Low pay and long hours at the *Observer* dictated Nowlan's holding down two or three jobs at once. A novel, *The Wanton Troopers,* written on a Canada Council grant in 1960 and not published until 1988, failed to rescue Nowlan from journalistic drudgery. Nowlan took a full-time position at the *Telegraph-Journal* in the more cosmopolitan Saint John, where he lived with his wife Claudine and their son John for the next five years. Successively reporter, provincial editor and night news editor for the *Telegraph-Journal,* Nowlan brings detailed first-hand knowledge to his poems about politics and current affairs. His sketch of Jamil Baroody, the Saudi ambassador to the UN, is keenly and dispassionately drawn:

> He tosses his pencil on the table
> (not as a symbol of anything but simply because he is through with it)
> and it bounces on the floor, out of reach, the first accident
> to occur here tonight, and he glances down,
> wondering where it fell, not because he cares
> but because it is human
> to glance down at things that have fallen.

Nowlan leads us beyond surfaces to the inner dignity of an old man in outworn service of "a king who still lives in the 14th century," a man whom Nowlan characterizes as "ignorant, cruel and bigoted as the rest of us." We sense in such description that Nowlan's interest in his subject extends far beyond the more obvious contradictions of which he has written incisively in the past—now he has begun to value and praise the mysterious polyphony that is the music inside each personality.

We notice also in this middle period of Nowlan a sudden and dramatic expansion of the poet's emotional range and response, accompanied by an enlargement of his stylistic repertoire. Now Nowlan works frequently in a more naturalistic Williams-influenced short line (occasionally in triads) and an expansive long line owing much to Whitman by way of Lawrence. A reporter by profession, and an increasingly public poet, Nowlan feels less compelled to remain hidden, to protectively divide public and private selves, now plunging into a world of far more subtle and complex oppositions. This marks the beginning of the poet's mature engagement with history, both past and contemporary, international as well as regional, in courageous poems grappling in their half-bemused, half-outraged way with the demonology of modern life:

> The newspapers speak of torture
> as though it were horseplay.
> This morning a picture of a Congolese rebel
> being kicked to death
> was captioned *the shoe is on the other foot*. . . .   ("In Our Time")

In 1966, Nowlan was diagnosed with thyroid cancer and underwent three major operations. This ordeal is chronicled in such unsparing poems as "In the Operating Room" and "Five Days in Hospital," in which the poet wrestles, Jacob-like, with his own death:

> I have discovered to my amazement
>   that I am unable to believe
>   in my own death.
> I know that I will die but I do not believe in it.
> Then how is it there are times
> when I am almost crazy with fear?   ("Five Days in Hospital")

The operations were successful and, although their severity probably contributed to Nowlan's death by weakening his system, he was to live another 17 years with no recurrence of the disease. According to Claudine Nowlan, the crisis had the positive effect of turning Nowlan's energy away from journalism and toward serious literary production.

As Robert Bly has emphasized in his introduction to *Playing the Jesus Game* (New Press, 1970), fear is a persistent theme throughout Nowlan's writing. If in the early poems Nowlan's project is to confront and exorcise fears of emotional and spiritual dismemberment in an environment hostile to the imagination, in the poems of the Sixties Nowlan faces the internalized enemy who manifests physically in the form of disease or, projected outward, becomes a murderer of others. His poem about the assassination of Martin Luther King, Jr., "The Night Editor's Poem," drives its dagger pitilessly into the part of us in unconscious collusion with impersonal forces that move against anyone attempting to liberate human beings. It is an honorable poem, one we in the United States could profit by knowing.

Nowlan's sixth poetry collection, *Bread, Wine and Salt,* won the 1967 Governor General's Award, the highest honor for poetry in Canada. The poems are a product of the enormous creative charge released by Nowlan's encounter with mortality and subsequent rededication to his art. While the early poems, for all their bravery and precision, are mostly "about" other people (albeit with Nowlan hovering behind them) in *Bread, Wine and Salt,* Nowlan reveals himself with disarming honesty and humor *as himself.* Nowlan knows he "contains multitudes," and his sense of the inner crowd and the difficulty of identifying a primary or "real" self among them reminds us at times of Neruda's playful orchestration of selves in *Extravagaria.*

In 1968, Alden Nowlan was appointed writer-in-residence at the University of New Brunswick in Fredericton, a post he was to occupy for the rest of his life. Freed from the economic necessity of having to divide his efforts between journalism and art, Nowlan produced five major books of poetry, from *The Mysterious Naked Man* (1969) to his late masterpiece *I Might Not Tell Everybody This* (1982). These were expansive years both artistically and socially, in which Nowlan's stature and influence as a literary figure grew to fit his accomplishment. He published a fine autobiographical novel, *Various Persons Named Kevin O'Brien,* short stories, drama, and essays, and the Nowlan household became a lively center for discussion of literature, politics, and culture.

The poems appearing near the end of Nowlan's life are those of a man who has, in Lawrence's phrase, "come through." The atmosphere of struggle with dread, depression and terror has for the most part lifted; a spiritual combat has been fought and largely won. A final fear has been recognized and confronted, one that Nowlan never names directly. The apparently light-hearted "In Praise of the Great Bull Walrus" offers a clue:

> I wouldn't like to be one
> of the walrus people

for the rest of my life
but I wish I could spend
one sunny afternoon
lying on the rocks with them.

Nowlan was a physically large man, and here he uses the walruses to gently caricature himself. (He has confessed in interviews a close identification with the bull moose in his popular early poem of that title; we may assume that behind any large animal in Nowlan is likely to stand the author's stout figure.) The poem concludes:

How good it is to share
the earth with such creatures
and how unthinkable it would have been
to have missed all this
by not being born:
a happy thought, that,
for not being born is
the only tragedy
that we can imagine
but need never fear.

By his own account in "It's Good to Be Here" ("There's quinine, she said. / That's bullshit, he told her."), Nowlan came near not being born at all. As a boy shamefully aware of being a less than "wanted" child, Nowlan took an uneasy and self-punishing refuge in fantasies of annihilation. In his novels, Nowlan describes his often hilarious adolescent power fantasies, but we must look to the poems for his brooding on a self-cancelling more extreme than suicide, as in "Afterword to Genesis" where Isaac experiences "an inexplicable eagerness / waiting to be blotted out, swallowed up, made nothing." The late poems enact Nowlan's decision to live despite the purely metaphysical and impossible yet inwardly oppressive threat of never-having-been.

Nowlan's final collection, *I Might Not Tell Everybody This,* is one of the best books published by a North American poet since mid-century. Its beauty and serenity are indicative of the author's having won through to a calm, human self-acceptance, a great achievement in an age defined by fear of the self projected outward onto others and nature. In these poems we hear Nowlan's peculiar music at its clearest and most fluid, the base a unique and haunting play of irony and tenderness, each giving way to promptings of the other. The overarching effect is of an uninterrupted and spontaneous conversation between what Yeats called "self and soul," the self who knows the world and its betrayals and the soul who longs ceaselessly for its impossible desires. We see the triumph of soul and desire especially in the love poems and in the poems written for Nowlan's son. That triumph distinguishes *I Might Not Tell Everybody This* as a whole, and is the source of light that plays over even the darker areas in these poems. In "Bobby Sands," we glimpse Nowlan's Irish great-great-grandmother Mary Foley who died in County Wexford "with green stains on her lips, with her hands filled with grass," while English wagons hauled away the Irish grain:

> . . . Being human, we
> each of us can bear no more than a particle
> of pain that is not our own; the rest is rhetoric.
> Better to shed a tear for Mary Foley
> than to rant or babble about suffering
> that is beyond our capacity to comprehend.
> And what of Bobby Sands? We talk too much,
> all of us. In common decency, don't speak
> of him unless you have gone at least a day
> without food, and be sure you understand
> that he loved being alive, the same as you.

The poem is both personal and rhetorical—Nowlan has learned to speak from private and public centers at once, blending the two tonalities with unmatched confidence and grace. The dividing line between the personal and the political, a sticking point in recent discussions of poetry, has disappeared; that is to say, the poem has become fully human.

At the height of his powers as a poet, Alden Nowlan died unexpectedly of respiratory failure in Fredericton in June, 1983.

* * *

Alden Nowlan is widely considered to be the most important literary figure to appear in the Maritime provinces in the past thirty years. Clearly Nowlan manages, in writing truthfully and artfully of his specific place, to travel far beyond merely provincial concerns and speak to and for a greater audience. His 1970 selection, *Playing the Jesus Game*, brought Nowlan to the attention of U.S. audiences midpoint in his writing career, but has long been out of print. The time is right for a new American selection drawing on the complete range of Alden Nowlan's poetry. The present volume, limited to 94 of his best poems, will serve to whet readers' appetites for more of this unjustly neglected poet's work and add to the demand, already heard in Canada, for a comprehensive collected edition.

Providing a brief critical and biographical glance at Alden Nowlan's life and work, I've hardly mentioned Nowlan's stunning technical ability, which the reader might easily miss in assuming these poems, so wonderfully conversational and direct, spilled effortlessly from the pen. We know that Nowlan labored over dozens of drafts of a poem to achieve the illusion of naturalness. Lest anyone doubt Nowlan's mastery, let them look carefully at "Waiting for Her" with its drumming, inwardly-screaming crescendo in the second stanza and its controlled quiet—equally anxious—in the third.

Another of Nowlan's gifts to us is his care for truth. Having labored most of his adult life in a profession now distrusted nearly as much as the politicians', Nowlan felt acutely the weight and expense of lies we live by, both the large, public ones and the smaller, private ones with which we comfort ourselves. He maintains a rigorous honesty, and in doing so communicates directly with some truth-organ in us that knows when it is or isn't being lied to. This discipline affords Nowlan a sophistication that places him light years ahead of many North American poets who persist in simple-minded antagonisms, assigning all evil to others. Reading Nowlan, one feels honored, as when reading Whitman, by the sheer human capacity for both good and evil (and the ability to choose between them) the poet has assumed for himself and his audience.

One measure of an artist's mastery is the extent to which we are made to care about his or her story. Alden Nowlan makes us care intensely about his story. Specific in its particulars, Nowlan's story partakes of some general struggle of the modern soul to surmount shame, poverty, powerlessness, and fear to enter the full richness of a human life. In this, Nowlan bears a striking resemblance to James Wright, who escaped the meanness of life in an Ohio factory town and in spite of personal hardship achieved the luminous gift of his poems. Both Nowlan and Wright identified profoundly with society's outcasts. Like Wright, Nowlan was constantly aware not only of the violence around him but of his own capacity for violence. The key, Nowlan suggests in poem after poem, is knowledge of self, as in "Confession," where, reflecting on the lust of a murderer-rapist, Nowlan tells his lover,

> [I] might love you less
> if I did not know
> that other one so well
> had not talked with him
> far into the night.

Visiting the Maritimes in 1989, six years after Nowlan's death, it became clear to me that many Canadians hold a Nowlan poem, such as "He Sits Down on the Floor of a School for the Retarded" or "Weakness," in a place of esteem similar to that reserved in the United States for a Wright poem such as "A Blessing" or "Lying in a Hammock at William Duffy's Farm in Pine Island, Minnesota."

The Canadian poet Robert Gibbs has described Nowlan's process—which applies not only to individual poems but to the general shape Nowlan's life and work took unfolding—as "a working through from self-esteem and self-doubt to an awareness of vanity and limitation in himself and others, and beyond that to a wider awareness lodged in compassion."[5] As difficult as Nowlan's circumstances undoubtedly were, alleviating his own suffering seems never to have been the final goal of his struggle as an artist or as a man. What is most beautiful in his poems, I think, is Nowlan's refusal, grounded in a sure knowledge of human moral limitations, to accept isolation and alienation, a refusal which leads him toward progressively deeper acts of compassion and generosity.

That isolation Nowlan fought to overcome has its natural breeding ground in small towns all over North America. I was a boy during the Fifties in a paper mill town in northern Wisconsin, in its way as hopeless and brutal as those Nowlan describes. In such places, one feels beneath the sun-lit surface of a cheerfully maintained normalcy a tremendous undertow of darkness: the bad luck, cruelty, disease, morbidity, and madness which rush into the vacuum created in the human community when a traditional culture rooted in place is left behind. Many in our time respond to this sense of threat by retreating into numbness, alcoholism, television, and "queer religions." Nowlan knows how difficult it is to maintain under such circumstances the alertness and openness that the practice of art requires.

That a mostly self-educated man without visible support in his early years should decisively overcome fear, confusion, and rage to produce, in nine full-length collections, one of the most deeply honest and humane bodies of poetry on our continent in this century is astonishing. In an era in which much North American poetry is dimmed by passivity, lack of desire, and a readiness to mock the hard-won achievements of past civilization, Alden Nowlan's poems demonstrate what is still possible when one has courage to face without denial the worst truths of our time and ourselves, and desire to honor the still deeper truths of the heart.

–Thomas R. Smith

NOTES

1. Alden Nowlan, "Growing Up in Katpesa Creek," in *Double Exposure*, p. 17, Brunswick Press, Fredericton, NB, 1978

2. Ted Jones, "Alden Nowlan: Required Reading," p. 12, *New Brunswick*, Vol. 8, No. 3-4, New Brunswick Information Service, Fredericton, NB, 1983

3. Lesley Choyce, "Interview," p. 3, *Pottersfield Portfolio*, Porters Lake, NS, Vol. 5, 1983-84

4. Ibid., p. 3

5. Robert Gibbs, "Introduction," p. xiv, in Alden Nowlan, *An Exchange of Gifts: Poems New and Selected*, Irwin Publishing, Toronto, 1985

The Bull Moose

POEMS FROM

The Rose and the Puritan
A Darkness in the Earth
Wind in a Rocky Country
Under the Ice
The Things Which Are
Five New Brunswick Poets

Beginning

From that they found most lovely, most abhorred,
my parents made me: I was born like sound
stroked from the fiddle to become the ward
of tunes played on the bear-trap and the hound.

Not one, but seven embraces they gave
each to the other, and he laid her down
the way the sun comes out. Oh, they were brave,
and then like looters in a burning town.

Their mouths left bruises, starting with the kiss
and ending with the proverb, where they stayed;
never in making was there brighter bliss,
followed by darker shame. Thus I was made.

The White Goddess

I being twelve and scared, my lantern shook,
shrunk to string my stomach knotted,
breathing the sultry mustiness of hay
and dung in the cowbarn,
and the heifer calving.

Ours was a windy country and its crops
were never frivolous, malicious rocks
kicked at the plough and skinny cattle broke
ditch ice for mud to drink and pigs were axed.

Finding the young bull drowned, his shoulders wedged
into a sunken hogshead in the pasture,
I vomited, my mother, yet the flies
around his dull eyes vanished with the kiss
your fingers sang into my hair all night.

Hens

Beside the horse troughs, General Grant
swaggered and foraged in the dry manure,
that winter we had twenty-seven hens
graced with white feathers and names of heroes.

Cock of the walk, he took the choicest fodder,
and he was totem, stud and constable
until his comb and spurs were frozen, bled,
and then the hens, quite calmly, pecked him dead.

Weakness

Old mare whose eyes
are like cracked marbles,
drools blood in her mash,
shivers in her jute blanket.

My father hates weakness worse than hail;
in the morning
        without haste
he will shoot her in the ear, once,
shovel her under in the north pasture.

Tonight
        leaving the stables,
he stands his lantern on an over-turned water pail,
turns,
        cursing her for a bad bargain,
and spreads his coat
carefully over her sick shoulders.

Flossie at School

Five laths in a cotton dress
was christened Flossie
and learned how to cry,
her eyes like wet daisies
behind thick glasses.

She was six grades ahead of me
and wore bangs; the big boys
called her "The Martian,"
they snowballed her home,
splashed her with their bicycles,
left horse dung in her coat pockets.

She jerked when anyone spoke to her,
and when I was ten
I caught up with her one day
on the way home from school,
and said, Flossie I really like you
but don't let the other kids know I told you,
they'd pick on me, but I do like you,
I really do, but don't tell anybody.
And afterwards I was ashamed
for crying when she cried.

Atlantis

No waves ten stories tall and terrible,
abrupt and hissing as a severed vein,
erased this city. First the rivers spilled
across our outer provinces, and then
there was some talk of dams, but most of us
approved of irrigation, anyhow
the peasants need a bath sometimes, we said,
and later when the swamps began to swell
and gulls were white against the misty sky,
the ancients said almost the same occurred
often when they were young, and so of course
we were ashamed to mention things like drips
we heard at night, and someone always laughed
when little men at parties claimed that pools
were rising slowly, slowly in their cellars.

Marian at the Pentecostal Meeting

Marian I cannot begrudge
    the carnival of God,
the cotton candy of her faith
    spun on a silver rod

to lick in bed; a peaked girl,
    neither admired nor clever,
Christ pity her and let her ride
    God's carousel forever.

Summer

It's summer yet but still the cold
coils through these fields at dusk, the gray Atlantic
haunting the hollows and a black bitch barking
between a rockpile and a broken fence
out on the hill a mile from town where maybe
a she-bear, groggy with blueberries, listens
and the colt, lonesome, runs in crooked circles.

God Sour the Milk of the Knacking Wench

God sour the milk of the knacking wench
with razor and twine she comes
to sanchion our blond and bucking bull,
pluck out his lovely plumbs.

God shiver the prunes on her bark of chest,
who capons the prancing young.
Let maggots befoul her alive in bed,
and dibble thorns in her tongue.

Gypsies

Jessie, my cousin, remembers there were gypsies
every spring, cat-eyes in smoky faces,
hair like black butter on leather laces.
Mothers on the high wagons whose babes sucked
flesh on O'Brien Street, I'd be ashamed.
The men stole everything and damned if they didn't
shrug if you caught them—giving back a hen
filched from your own coop like a gift to a peasant.
The little girls danced, their red skirts winking,
their legs were lovely, greasy as drumsticks.
And they kidnapped children. Oh, every child
hoped secretly to be stolen by gypsies.

Cousins

My cousins, the kind
of family who in another time
and place took to brigandage
for the hell of it,

so violent they go logging
or harvesting their meager acres
as if they were going on a raid,
work twelve hours, then hitch-hike to a dance
in Larchmont or Bennington,
get drunk as a fiddler's bitch,
roostering for skirts and fist-fights;

and when one of them
gets a girl in trouble,
which is inevitable,
he marries her,

it's a point of honor
with them to treat their wives
like whores, they talk about bedding
them as they talk
about going to the privy,

they are so afraid
of weakness, my cousins
who are not frightened
by boots or tire-irons
behind the dance hall in Bennington
are scared into hilarity and contempt by kisses.

My Father

My father never takes
anything for granted–
food, shelter, sleep,
he is always grateful.

He lives alone now,
when he opens the pantry
he always acts amazed
that there is bacon and flour.

He eats slowly
surprised there's enough
finishes wiping
the plate out with bread.

He is seldom happy
but I never saw a man
so content with small comforts:

wife, children gone
there is nothing left–

I know he could curl up
in his mackinaw
on his own barnfloor
and sleep thankful
at being allowed to rest there.

Baptism

In summer-colored dresses, six young girls
are walking in the river; they look back,
frightened and proud; a choir and a cloud
of starlings sing; in rubber boots and black
frock-coat the preacher bends them separately
under; since the up-rushing stream expands
their skirts as they go down he closes them
each time with gently disapproving hands.

Sunday Afternoon

In the next house they're punishing a child.
Violently too: the boy is being whipped
with something limber that thwacks like applause,
water that's stoned or cotton when it's ripped.

All three are yelling. Though the boy
uses no proscribed idioms, it's plain
he's cursing manfully. But also begging–
defiant yet obsequious in pain.

The mother's inconsistent too, she wants
the boy whipped, obviously, but she hates
the man for beating him. So she exhorts
the son vindictively and still berates

the father's harshness. He a normal man
playing a role he loathes, a prisoner,
expresses his abhorrence of the whole
mess by applying himself to it harder.

Homebrew

Molasses, oranges and yeast
purchased with promises and mixed at night,
the keg buried in steaming dung
to hasten fermentation, then the wait
for some excuse to fork it out
(a rainy day, the mill not running);
the men in their sawdust-covered denims
sitting on blocks of pressed hay in the barn
and drinking from a single mug, their thumbs
spooning out shreds of hay and frequently
flies and then bolting it, holding their breath,
and spitting afterwards, grunting their pleasure.

Andy Shaw

Three generations (and he loathed them all)
	bought meat from Andy Shaw who clerked for Etter,
working six days a week for thirty years,
	hating his job and looking for a better.

He never married and he blamed his wage,
	never went more than twenty miles from town;
and every year came earlier to work,
	cursing the butcher shop that tied him down.

When Charley Etter died his son came home
	to run the store, so Andy got his pay.
Some claim the old man cried, offered to work
	for less—or nothing—if they'd let him stay.

Warren Pryor

When every pencil meant a sacrifice
his parents boarded him at school in town,
slaving to free him from the stony fields,
the meager acreage that bore them down.

They blushed with pride when, at his graduation,
they watched him picking up the slender scroll,
his passport from the years of brutal toil
and lonely patience in a barren hole.

When he went in the Bank their cups ran over.
They marvelled how he wore a milk-white shirt
work days and jeans on Sundays. He was saved
from their thistle-strewn farm and its red dirt.

And he said nothing. Hard and serious
like a young bear inside his teller's cage,
his axe-hewn hands upon the paper bills
aching with empty strength and throttled rage.

Christ

Aloft in a balsam fir I watched Christ go,
two crows in that same tree made human laughter.

He clambered over the log fence and crossed
the orange-yellow field, his purple skirts

swishing the grain and I could hear that sound,
so close he was, and separate the hairs

in his red beard. He passed beneath me, never
once looking up, and having reached the gate

to the hill pasture shrank smaller and smaller
becoming first a fist and then a finger

and then a fleck of purple on the hillside.
At last, at the edge of the wood, he vanished altogether.

St. John River

The color of a bayonet this river
that glitters blue and solid on the page
in tourist folders, yet some thirty towns
use it as a latrine, the sewerage
seeping back to their wells, and farmers maddened
by debt or queer religions winter down
under the ice, the river bottom strewn
with heaps of decomposing bark torn loose
from pulpwood driven south, its acid juice
killing the salmon. August, when the stink
of the corrupted water floats like gas
along these streets, what most astonishes
is that the pictures haven't lied, the real
river is beautiful, as blue as steel.

The Mark

The mark is on me.
As I approach the liquor store
the winos emerge from the alley
thrust out their quivering palms,
like cripples accosting Christ.

And I give them money:
a quarter for a pint of beer,
ten cents toward a shot of rum.
"You know what it's like," they say.
"You know what it's like."

Imagining the taste,
the cool of it on the tongue.
Oh God, the first
little glimmer of warmth
in the stomach, and then

the stones softening, the flutes,
the incorruptible body,
Marsyas challenging Apollo–

yes, brothers,
I know what it's like.
I know.

Party at Bannon Brook

At the dead end of a road twisting snake-like
as that out of Eden, in a hunting camp, the hoarse creek crawling
through the closed door like the wet ghost of some drowned Adam
coughing water on the floor, I sprawl on a straw-filled bunk
and drink rum with strangers:

The chef in his tall white hat
and apron embroidered
with ribald slogans
spears steaks with slivers
of white pine, roaring.

Beside me, in the leaping shadows
next the rough boards of the wall, her head
resting on a calendar from which all the months
have been ripped away, leaving only
the likeness of a woman
with orange skin and a body that might have been
stretched on a rack in the dungeon
of Gilles de Rais, it has such perverse,
blasphemous proportions, a girl sits, swaying
in time with the chef's song, her sweater
pulled out at the back, my circular arm
stroking the soft fat
of her belly—not because I love her
but because I am afraid. If we could do what we wish,
always, I would tell them I understand:
this is the season
when the bobcat is not driven away
by smoke, and the eagle
makes reconnaissance from the coast.

But they will not listen.
And they could do worse: tomorrow
the chef will be cashiered, kill eight hours
sending bills to debtors and this girl
sit at a desk, addressing letters
to the brains of dead men, each a packaged pudding
shelved in cold storage, and I

in whom despair
has bred superior cunning
will escape only by long study
of how the silver beads turn to gold, falling
by my employer's window, the icicles
stroked by an amorous sun.

The Bull Moose

Down from the purple mist of trees on the mountain,
lurching through forests of white spruce and cedar,
stumbling through tamarack swamps,
came the bull moose
to be stopped at last by a pole-fenced pasture.

Too tired to turn or, perhaps, aware
there was no place left to go, he stood with the cattle.
They, scenting the musk of death, seeing his great head
like the ritual mask of a blood god, moved to the other end
of the field, and waited.

The neighbors heard of it, and by afternoon
cars lined the road. The children teased him
with alder switches and he gazed at them
like an old, tolerant collie. The women asked
if he could have escaped from a Fair.

The oldest man in the parish remembered seeing
a gelded moose yoked with an ox for plowing.
The young men snickered and tried to pour beer
down his throat, while their girl friends took their pictures.

And the bull moose let them stroke his tick-ravaged flanks,
let them pry open his jaws with bottles, let a giggling girl
plant a little purple cap
of thistles on his head.

When the wardens came, everyone agreed it was a shame
to shoot anything so shaggy and cuddlesome.
He looked like the kind of pet
women put to bed with their sons.

So they held their fire. But just as the sun dropped in the river
the bull moose gathered his strength
like a scaffolded king, straightened and lifted his horns
so that even the wardens backed away as they raised their rifles.
When he roared, people ran to their cars. All the young men
leaned on their automobile horns as he toppled.

The Shack Dwellers

Most of them look
as though their bodies were boneless.

Every animal
has its own defense:
theirs is plasticity.

Kick them in the face
and nothing breaks.
It's as if your boot
sank in wet dough.

But sometimes a trick
of hunger or heredity
gives one small bones
like an aristocrat's,
transparent skin
and delicate, blue veins.

You'll see one of the lost
Bourbons or Romanoffs,
dirty toes protruding
from the holes in his sneakers,
a hint of the old
hauteur in his hawk nose
as he tries to talk the grocer
out of a roll of bologna
and a loaf of stale bread.

Stoney Ridge Dance Hall

They don't like strangers.
So be careful how you smile.

Eight generations
of Hungerfords, McGards and Staceys
have lived on this ridge
like incestuous kings.
Their blood is so pure
it will not clot.

This is the only
country they know.
There are men here
who have never heard of Canada.

When they tire of dancing
they go down the road
and drink white lightning
out of the bung
of a molasses puncheon.

But they never forget
to strap on the knuckles
they've made from beer bottle
caps and leather

and there are sharp spikes
in their orange logging boots.

The Grove Beyond the Barley

This grove is too secret: one thinks of murder.
Coming upon your white body (for as yet
I do not know you, therefore have no right
to speak of discovering
you, can address myself
to your body only) seeing the disorder
of your naked limbs, the arms outstretched
like one crucified, the legs bent like a runner's,
it took me less than a second to write a novel:
the husband in the black suit
worn at his wedding, the hired man
in his shirt the color
of a rooster's comb and, in the end, you
thrown here like an axed colt.
Then I saw your breasts: they are not asleep,
move like the shadows of leaves
stirred by the wind. I hope you do not waken,
before I go; one who chooses
so dark a place
to lie naked
might cry out. The shadows quicken,
I wish you a lover,
dreams of sunlit meadows,
imagine myself a gentle satyr.

The Execution

On the night of the execution
a man at the door
mistook me for the coroner.
"Press," I said.

But he didn't understand. He led me
into the wrong room
where the sheriff greeted me:
"You're late, Padre."

"You're wrong," I told him. "I'm Press."
"Yes, of course, Reverend Press."
We went down a stairway.

"Ah, Mr. Ellis," said the Deputy.
"Press!" I shouted. But he shoved me
through a black curtain.
The lights were so bright
I couldn't see the faces
of the men sitting
opposite. But, thank God, I thought
they can see me!

"Look!" I cried. "Look at my face!
Doesn't anybody know me?"

Then a hood covered my head.
"Don't make it harder for us," the hangman whispered.

Edna

She's got the right eyes
and the separate laughs,
the silly, on-purpose one
she gives to adults,
the wise, just-happens one
she keeps to herself.

Too bad God
in letting her be eight forever
didn't remember
to stop all the clocks
at the same time

so that instead of
those mildewed ropes
bursting out of
elastic stockings

she had hopscotch legs
that go in all directions
at once,
and the funny kind of beauty
we try to meet
with gentle laughter.

Sometimes

Sometimes, not often, I wish there were only
the clean rapture of the body. I wish I could go
into a strange place, an amnesiac, and find that she too
had forgotten history.
                                                  Oh, love is good
but it reaches out
to take in the stars,
runs backwards and forwards. Sometimes I wish
for a world no bigger than the coupling bodies
of two clockless strangers.
                                                  But when I seek it,
she makes some small gesture—puts her hand to her hair—and I can tell
she has not forgotten herself, that she tries to please me
for some purpose of her own, and I almost weep; or she murmurs
some private word, and I curse myself and berate her.

Love Poem for Therese

We asked too much
of one another,

broken, looked
to the broken for wholeness.

That truth we shared today.

And this also: perhaps, there is no one.
Perhaps all are broken: three billion dolls
leaking sawdust. Heat, light and power
shut off in the forgotten warehouse.

No wonder, you threw yourself in my arms and wept!
No wonder, I whispered all
the old love names as I clung to you.

Waiting for Her

Waiting for her,
rain on the windshield,
cars passing,
their tires hissing
on the black pavement;

one minute the rain
pounding the car roof
as drummers
must have pounded
their drums at old executions,
with their fists,
not wanting to hear the screams;

the next minute
so quiet
I can hear my cigarette
burning when I inhale.

I listen
for her, I know how
she walks at night
and in the rain, with a different rhythm.

I brace myself to pretend
if she comes I was sure she'd come,
if she doesn't that I don't care.

Canadian Love Song

Your body's a small word with many meanings.
Love. If. Yes. But. Death.
Surely I will love you a little while,
perhaps as long as I have breath.

December is thirteen months long,
July's one afternoon; therefore,
lovers must outwit wool,
learn how to puncture fur.

To my love's bed, to keep her warm,
I'll carry wrapped and heated stones.
That which is comfort to the flesh
is sometimes torture to the bones.

Glance Down at Things That Have Fallen

POEMS FROM

Bread, Wine and Salt
Playing the Jesus Game
The Mysterious Naked Man
Between Tears and Laughter

I, Icarus

There was a time when I could fly. I swear it.
Perhaps, if I think hard for a moment, I can even tell you the year.
My room was on the ground floor at the rear of the house.
My bed faced a window.
Night after night I lay on my bed and willed myself to fly.
It was hard work, I can tell you.
Sometimes I lay perfectly still for an hour before I felt
    my body rising from the bed.
I rose slowly, slowly until I floated three or four feet
    above the floor.
Then, with a kind of swimming motion, I propelled myself
    toward the window.
Outside, I rose higher and higher, above the pasture fence,
    above the clothesline, above the dark, haunted trees
    beyond the pasture.
And, all the time, I heard the music of flutes.
It seemed the wind made this music.
And sometimes there were voices singing.

Midnight of the First Snow

Midnight of the first snow.
In the open pasture
the cattle pause,
lift up their heads
with a little stir of wonder,
then go back to grazing,
getting every blade within reach
before taking
another sleepy step in the darkness.

And He Wept Aloud So That the Egyptians Heard It

In my grandfather's house
for the first time in years,
houseflies big as bumblebees
playing crazy football
in the skim-milk-colored windows,

leap-frogging from
the cracked butter saucer
to our tin plates of
rainbow trout and potatoes, catching the bread
on its way to our mouths,
      mounting one another
      on the rough deal table.

It was not so much their filth
as their numbers and persistence and—
oh, admit this, man, there's no point in poetry
if you withhold the truth
once you've come by it—
      their symbolism:
      Baal-Zebub,
god of the poor and outcast,

that enraged me, made me snatch the old man's
Family Herald, attack them like a maniac,
lay to left and right until the window sills
overflowed with their smashed corpses,
until bits of their wings
stuck to my fingers,
until the room buzzed with their terror. . . .

And my grandfather, bewildered, and afraid,
came to help me:
    "never seen a year
    when the flies were so thick"
as though he'd seen them at all before I came!

His voice so old and baffled and pitiful
that I threw my club into the wood box and sat down
    and wanted to beg his forgiveness
as we ate on in silence broken only
by the almost inaudible humming
of the flies rebuilding their world.

Britain Street

Saint John, New Brunswick

This is a street at war.
The smallest children
battle with clubs
till the blood comes,
shout "fuck you!"
like a rallying cry–

while mothers shriek
from doorsteps and windows
as though the very names
of their young were curses:

"Brian! Marlene!
Damn you! God damn you!"

or waddle into the street
to beat their own with switches:
"I'll teach you, Brian!
I'll teach you, God damn you!"

On this street,
even the dogs
would rather fight
than eat.

I have lived here nine months
and in all that time
have never once heard
a gentle word spoken.

I like to tell myself
that is only because
gentle words are whispered
and harsh words shouted.

In Those Old Wars

In those old wars
where generals wore yellow ringlets
and sucked lemons at their prayers,
other things being equal
the lost causes were the best.

Lee rode out of history
on his gray horse, Traveller,
so perfect a hero
had he not existed
it would have been necessary to invent him—
war stinks without gallantry.

An aide, one of the few who survived,
told him,
Country be damned, general,
for six months these men
have had no country but you.
They fought barefoot
and drank blueberryleaf tea.

The politicians
strung up Grant
like a carrot,
made him a Merovingian.
They stole everything,
even the coppers from Lincoln's dead eyes.

In those days, the vanquished
surrendered their swords like gentlemen,
the victors alone
surrendered their illusions.
The easiest thing to do for a Cause
is to die for it.

In Our Time

The newspapers speak of torture
as though it were horseplay.
This morning a picture of a Congolese rebel
being kicked to death
was captioned *the shoe is on the other foot*
and a story from Saigon
told of a Viet Cong prisoner
who complained of thirst
being *overwhelmed by the hospitality*
of his captors
who cheerfully refreshed him
and also his memory
by pumping a generous quantity of water
through rubber tubes into his nostrils.

On Hearing of the Death of Dr. William Carlos Williams

For Sandy Ives

I am glad I did not read of his death
until after a friend telephoned
from another country
and told me drunkenly:
"The old man is dead
and I wanted to talk
to someone who would understand."
I am glad, too, I was drunk enough
that the two of us could sit,
side by side, on the cross bar of a telephone pole
midway between
Orono, Maine, and Hartland, New Brunswick,
dangle our feet in the sky
and drink to the memory
of an old man who took too long to die
because he had never learned
how the trick was done.

A Mug's Game

At the party that followed the poetry reading,
one girl kept telling me how thrilled she was to meet
someone who hadn't gone to university, and another said
I reminded her so much of whoever it was who played
in *Bus Stop* she kept expecting Marilyn to walk in, and the hostess
extending three bite-size salami sandwiches
and a glass of warm whiskey and ginger ale
smiled at me like Li'l Abner's Aunt Bessie
welcoming her nephew to Toronto.

The man from the CBC, who said: "Of course, you're staying
at the YMCA" and thought he was humoring me
by acting impressed when he found out I wasn't,

explained: "The purpose of such readings is to give writers
from unlikely places like Hartland, New Brunswick,
the chance to communicate
with others
of their own kind."

The Knife

I do not know
where this knife began
nor how many times
it has travelled over the world.
But this I know, my love:

Earlier today I was not applauded
by a man whom I hate and this because
I bungled a job I neither
wanted nor understood.

And a man plucks out
steel from his own flesh,
even when he knows
this blade goes
always from breast to breast.

I am not always brave
enough to keep
such knives in my body.
And so now I stab you, my love,
drive it in hard,
twist it in deep.

The Word

Though I have the gift of tongues
and can move mountains,
my words are nothing
compared with yours,
though you only
look up from my arms
and whisper my name.

This is not pride
because I know
it is not
my name that you whisper
but a sign
between us,
like the word
that was spoken
at the beginning
of the world
and will be spoken again
only when the world ends.

This is not that word
but the other
that must be spoken
over and over
while the world lasts.

Tears,
laughter,
a lifetime!
All in one word!

The word you whisper
when you look up
from my arms
and seem to say
my name.

Day's End

For Anne

I have worked since daylight in the hayfields.
We walked home at dusk, following the horses.
For supper, I ate hot bread and spiced ham,
        onions and tomatoes.
Now I kneel over a basin of cold water
and a woman washes my hair—
a strong woman whose knuckles rake my scalp.
Her hands smell of soap, I am naked to the waist,
        she leans her weight against me;
laughs huskily when I seize her wrists
        and try to push away her hands.
I am young and strong but a great weariness is upon me—
I would be willing to die now if I were sure that death is sleep.

Five Days in Hospital

1 I have come beyond fear to a place where there is almost
silence,
except now I am all the numbers
on all the clocks in the world:
things are broken apart,
I am the ruins of a crystal man
and there are no sentences
but only words. . . .

2 I have discovered to my amazement
that I am unable to believe
in my own death.
I know that I will die but I do not believe in it.
Then how is it there are times
when I am almost crazy with fear?

3 I look *in* at the world
like a ghost startled by the sight
of his own body
lying quite apart from him
in this bed. . . .

4 Where do flames go when they go out?
They go back to the sun.
How do they get there?
Like a flight of birds with bright feathers
flying south through the black
morning . . .

5 Fear of deafness has stopped my ears.
Fear of blindness has sewn up my eyes.
Fear of nakedness has stripped me bare.
Fear of the desert has made me abjure drink.
Yet even now, bad joke for a black morning,
fear of silence has not stilled my tongue.

In the Operating Room

The anesthetist is singing
"Michael, row the boat ashore,
Hallelujah!"
And I am astonished
that his arms
are so hairy—
thick, red, curly hair
like little coppery ferns
growing out of
his flesh
from wrist
to shoulder.
I would like
to reach up
and touch
the hairy arm
of the anesthetist
because it may be
the last living thing
I will ever see
and I am glad
it is not
white and hairless
—but if I reached up
and wound
a few wisps
of his hair
around my forefinger
as I would like to do
they would think
their drugs
had made me silly
and might remember

and laugh
if I live,
so I concentrate
very hard
on the song
the anesthetist
is singing–
"The River Jordan
is muddy and cold,
Hallelujah!"
And soon
everything
is dark
and nothing
matters
and when I try
to reach up
and touch
the hair
which I think of
now as
little jets
of fire,
I discover
they've strapped
my arms
to the table.

Escape from Eden

When I was near death,
these little nurses
stripped me naked
and bathed me.
When it appeared
I would live,
they covered
my loins
with a sheet.
When I learned to sit up
and drink consommé
through a straw,
they somehow managed
to wash my back
without removing
my pajama jacket.
Now that I can walk
to the sink and back
without falling,
they knock loudly,
pause,
before slowly opening
the door
of my room.

Confession

Beloved, it frightens me
how all things circle and meet.

I have singled you out
from all the world.

When you lie naked beneath me
or when only our fingertips
touch on the street,
I love you so gently
I become a saint
and would preach to the birds,
had they no better music.

Yet nothing is simple:
all things circle and meet.

The man who took his pleasure
of the young girl's body
and then strangled her
and threw her in a sewer
like a used condom—

there was a moment
before he gave way
to terror
when he studied her knees
like a famished boy,

an instant when he noted
how the spring wind
played with her hair
like young deer in a wheatfield
(he too was a sentimentalist)

and I, beloved,
lightly kissing your breasts
(do you remember, my little jester,
how you told me once
to be less gentle
with the sacred grotto
between your thighs
because, darling, it won't break)

might love you less
if I did not know
that other so well
had not talked with him
far into the night.

Witness to Murder

The cameraman must be running backwards
in front of the soldiers and their prisoner
who wears black shorts and a sportshirt
imprinted with sunflowers and daisies
and has sandals on his feet
and does not look as if he understands
that he is about to die.
But we know
he would not be there on the screen
unless something horrible
were in store for him.
And I hear myself talking
to his picture, as I haven't talked
to a picture since I was ten:
Make a run for it! I shout.
There's a chance you'll make it.
Grab for a gun, maybe you'll take
one of the bastards with you.
But he can't hear me.
He keeps on walking.

Golf

My friends believe in golf, address the ball,
however bent, to an appointed place.
Newtonians, convinced no orb can fall
out of the numbered course of time and space.

But I, from clumsiness or pity, drive
balls out of bounds and into woods and traps,
my knees and wrists vindictive in their love
for dark and tangled places not on maps.

"Golf's not your game," they say. But I persist.
"Next one goes straight. . . ." I promise. Oh, they're fooled
right cunningly by my secretive wrist
that treacherously lets the world go wild.

Let them attack the green. As for myself,
I pitch into the darkness, like a wolf.

The Dog Returned from the Woods

After three days the dog came home, a stranger,
slinking along the footpath from the hills,
drawn by a sullen truce of thirst and hunger,
his muzzle visored in porcupine quills.

The children saw him first and yelled his name
or rather the name of the dog who'd gone:
"Peter!" As if so wild a beast would come—
"Peter!" might have been "death" for all he knew.

And then they saw the difference in his walk,
a strangeness far more terrible than pain,
a wild thing lapping at the cattle trough,
his black lips oozing blood and the red stain
floating like ribbon in the water. Hurt
and baffled by his treachery they scowled,
wanting to weep, and he, his grim thirst met,
threw back his quill-bewhiskered head and howled.

The People Who Are Gone

In the days of the people who are gone—that was the way
the old people began their stories, Peter Little Bear says,
and now, well, those story tellers they've gone too.
Until the white man came we had no history
and now we have nothing else.
            But in the old days,
in the days of the people who are gone (he grins because
even though we're friends he still needs
that grin to escape through
should I suddenly betray him
and it's a weapon too that he can use
if I ask more than he's able to give.)
            In the old days, then,
every one of our boys when he came to a certain age
was sent into the woods alone to talk with God.
They fasted, I guess, and I don't think they were allowed
to take any weapons. The men may even have done
things to them before they went. I don't know. But every one
when he got to be, oh, thirteen or fourteen, had to go
into the woods and wait for God to come
down from the sun or out of the trees. So every man
had spoken with God, face to face.
            —And what did he say, I ask, their God I mean?
I don't know, Peter says. Maybe they never told,
maybe he only said hello
in Maliseet. My Gosh, if God himself
spoke to you would you remember what he said
and would it matter if you did?
And, gently this time,
Peter grins again.

The Fat Man's Poem

A fat man is lying on a bed in a furnished room in Pimlico.
He is writing with a mechanical pencil on a sheet torn from
        a child's exercise book.
His writing board is a magazine—at intervals he doodles
        spectacles and mustaches on Elizabeth Taylor,
        Richard Burton and three anonymous models
clad in made-in-America sweaters of washable orlon.

He props himself up on an elbow and writes:
In those days I was as innocent as one of the legendary child-saints.
Then, after a pause: *But aren't innocence and sainthood incompatible?*

He lights a cigarette and, from habit, because he has always been poor
counts those left in the package.
He wishes he were a painter or a singer,
how he covets the hands and eyes of Paul Klee,
how jealous he is, sometimes, of applause and money—
though he is thirty-two years old
he plays records with his eyes shut
and pretends it is he who is singing!

So this is one of those who would change the world!
He is very disgusted with himself today
because he has waited for the voices
and they haven't come
        (*pretentious balderdash* he scribbles on his sheet of paper).

Then, suddenly, he writes:
A fat man is lying on a bed in a furnished room in Pimlico.
Soon his pencil is racing across the paper;
and he forgets about cigarettes, forgets about everything,
until it is finished
and he reads what he has written
and doesn't know whether to be proud or ashamed.

For Jamil Baroody

Saudi Arabian ambassador to the United Nations,
on the occasion of his address to the Security Council, June, 1967

He tosses his pencil on the table
(not as a symbol of anything but simply because he is through with it)
and it bounces on the floor, out of reach, the first accident
to occur here tonight, and he glances down,
wondering where it fell, not because he cares
but because it is human
to glance down at things that have fallen.

He interrupts his speech, which is not a speech after all,
but the monologue of a man who, it is apparent,
has made many speeches in his time
but is old now and, perhaps, already childish,
speaks to the Russian beside him, says something
that makes the others laugh
not because it is funny
but because it is the kind of thing
an old man says to a younger.

The Russian nods and smiles. He is a little nervous
about what the old man may say next
and a little amused and there is even
a hint of affection.
For the first time
I believe the Russian
really likes Chinese poetry, bow ties and pipe tobacco.
I am even prepared to believe he has laughed
until the neighbors banged on the wall
and that once, long ago,
he cried himself to sleep.

But forget the Russian. He could be replaced by a computer
programmed in Moscow, and the others are no better,
endlessly exchanging their mimeographed resolutions
while, somewhere else, drunken gods shoot dice
to decide whether or not to continue history.

Listen to this one old man, apologist for slavery,
servant of a king who still lives in the 14th century,
one who, I have little doubt,
truly believes that his Prophet's corpse
revived, mounted a white horse
and leapt from the Rock of Abraham into Paradise;
a man as ignorant, cruel and bigoted as the rest of us.

Laid bare so innocently, even his weaknesses
possess a kind of grandeur,
as when he forgets he's supposed to leave
the table when he's finished speaking
and has trouble understanding the little aide sent to remind him,
finally gets to his feet, makes a slight but very formal bow
toward the diplomats who already are listening
to someone reading a long statement about something else
and walks away with the smile
of an old man forgiving his own stupidity.

Afterword to Genesis

"Let us hasten away before He changes His mind again," the
Patriarch said as he cleaned his knife on a handful
of leaves and grass.

And they came down to the tents as quickly as the old man's
infirmities would allow, not looking back for fear He had
chosen to follow them.

And later men were assigned to drag branches over the hoofprints
of the caravan,

and to leave meat at the site of every encampment, covering
it over with stones so that the birds and animals could not
defile it.

Yet the time came when the young man, Isaac, could not sleep
for remembering

how he had been made less than a woman, less than a child,
less than a slave

how he had stood perfectly still like an animal,

how he had trembled with fear and an inexplicable eagerness

waiting to be blotted out, swallowed up, made nothing.

A Mime for Lovers

They are facing one another
in a little clearing
in the jungle
and have exchanged
all the words and signs
of greeting:
he has held out his hands to show her
they are empty
and she is very careful
not to touch a stone
or stick she could lift,
so careful, in fact,
that he's becoming
suspicious of her motives
—why does she keep looking away
from that rock near her feet?
Has he misjudged her, after all?
His eyes narrow. He hesitates,
then decides to take a chance.
He hands her the smallest of his knives
and waits to see what she will do with it.
The blade is small. At worst she can only
scar him.
She smiles. They
smile at one another.
Slowly,
so he will not misunderstand,
she takes a handful
of arrows from
her quiver and drops them
at his feet.

A Tiger in the Dublin Zoo

Know that I am Napoleon, the great, the magnificent tiger.
Observe how an emperor
takes possession of the ground
on which he stands, imposes his own order
on the space around him.
                                        I walk to and fro,
                                        and am never halted.
I stop and turn where I choose.
                                                    And that
is three feet short
of the end of the cage.
                                      No more and no less.
Never once have I forgotten myself
              and been stopped by the bars.
I am Napoleon, the great, the magnificent tiger.

Poem for George Frederick Clarke

Once again the act as metaphor
                                        solidifies,
I feel
        the laying on of hands,
                                        reading
the inscription in an old book
given me today by an old man
who has written:
                        I have drunk deep from this;
                        now it is your turn to drink, and to keep.
There is more
                    underneath
                                    in Latin.
And it is not
                    in the least important
that I can't translate it.
                                For I know what it means.
It was his generation's
way of transforming
an occasion into
a ceremony.
                And I wish
I knew some equally grand and simple
response,
            certain words or gestures
expressing love with such
                                    dignity, yes
and such reticence.

Cornflowers

I am a saint with a broken wing
who shakes his fists like the wind.
You
are the homecoming
of the sun,
an hurrah of grass.
The cornflowers are not yet
aware they will die soon
from last night's frost.
They are like the Empress
Elizabeth of Austria
who was stabbed with a blade so thin
she continued to smile
and did not interrupt
her walk,
although it had pierced her heart.
Since in this place and season
they are the only flowers
that do not ask for money
I give you them.
Nothing else is beautiful
this hunchbacked October night
except the moon.

He Raids the Refrigerator and Reflects on Parenthood

Nowlan, you maudlin boob,
almost blubbering because
two hours ago at the party
your son said, I'll be
fifteen tomorrow, can I
have a whole pint of beer?
Grinning so he could say
it was a joke if you
took it that way; but he
was serious all right:
it's like music sometimes
how serious he can be
about small matters
which you're thereby
reminded were
important.
                    And you hesitated,
not because you ever
considered refusing
but because you wanted him
to know that you, too,
value rituals. But
there were only enough
cool ones for the guests.
So you gave him a warm one.
It doesn't matter, he said.
It's okay. But of course it did.
The rite was spoiled
by an imperfection. And now he's
asleep upstairs and you're
holding open the door
of the refrigerator, contemplating
a pint bottle with no more

than two ounces taken from it
and the cap put back so well
you'd need an opener
to take it off again, thinking
of the petty treason
we commit so often
against those we love,
the confidence games
in which parents play
their children for suckers.

The Night Editor's Poem

A child is lost near a lake
in the woods outside the city;
a man has been found dead
in a hotel and our reporter knows only
that the detectives have sent out
for sandwiches and coffee which
they're now consuming
in the same room with the corpse and a woman
who may be a suspect,
if there has been a murder, although right now
it looks more like suicide,
in which case our photographer
should get out of there as fast as he can
because nobody remembered to arrange for a picture
of the new officers of the Knights of Pythias.
There is flooding
in the Upper St. John River Valley and a cabbie
has been stabbed in Fredericton, and Trudeau
looks like a shoo-in unless
there's a deal, which would mean
we'd have to pull the lead editorial and kill
that display of cuts
on page five, and we should do something
on page one about Vietnam, although all there is
so far is the usual round-up
that nobody reads and

Bulletin,
Martin Luther King has been shot
in Memphis, the extent of
his injuries has not yet
been determined.

I send the kid
for a one column, head and shoulders,
cut, and ask if there've been any deaths
from the floods, because if there haven't been
I can shove that story downpage
and do a two column upper left
display on King unless,
                    Bulletin,
                    his injuries
                    are critical,
and I push everything down
four inches and send the kid
for a one and one-half columns,
head and shoulders, not more than three
inches deep,
            and there's a call from the hotel,
our reporter sounding disappointed
because, sure enough, it was suicide
and that means only three inches
of type on the back page, and
by the time Mac got to the Pythian Castle
they'd gone home but maybe we have a file cut
of the grand chancellor
we can use on provincial; there's a hell of a good
shot of the mother
of the lost child taken when they told her
they'd found the body, one that will stand up
in three columns with everything but her face
cropped out, something good enough
to send out on the wire and,
                    Bulletin,
                    Martin Luther King
                    is dead,

and it's too late
for a wirephoto which means
dig out that shot of him being hit
by a stone in Chicago, I think it was,
and have the engraver mask it so
nothing shows except
his body falling, and we'll set the story
in 12-point boldface, 18 ems, under
an all-caps 72-point Headline Gothic
head and splash it across
the top half of page one,
and it's not until later,
hours later,
eating ham and eggs
at an all-night diner,
shrugging my shoulders
to work some of the ache
out of them,
that I pick up the paper
again and understand
that Martin Luther King
is dead, and that I care.

Excerpt from

That Year on Salisbury Street

Every night except Saturday I climbed those stairs and
every night as I stopped to take my key from my pocket
I heard the Fischers quarrelling.
Her voice was shrill; I could distinguish most of the words.
His was a rumble; I could make out a word only here and
there.
Sometimes I thought of her as The Fife, and of him as The Drum.
You bastard, said The Fife, telling me you were a foreman!
I found out what kind of foreman you are!
A roll of drums.
You're not a man! You're an old woman! Are you listening
to me, you son of a bitch?
A roll of drums.
Her voice changed occasionally to a hoarse whisper, presumably
when she remembered that the occupants of the other flats
were probably listening. Sometimes a neighbor pounded
on the wall or yelled through the partition
for them to shut up, for God's sake, don't you know what
time it is? Then there was a brief silence, broken by
the whisper that became louder and louder until she was
almost screaming again.
Perhaps she wants him to beat her, I used to conjecture,
standing there with my key and flashlight. Perhaps she
wants him to beat her but is ashamed to tell him so.
She's furious because he's too stupid to divine what
she wants from him.
Perhaps she even wants him to kill her. Or perhaps she
knows that he wants her to beat him or kill him and
she hates him for it.
But I never found out the answer; although two or three
weeks after they left the police came around asking
questions about them.

He Takes His Leave

It was as if I'd opened
Grimms' Fairy Tales and lowered myself into
one of the illustrations, become
the stripling taking his leave
of his village, on foot, with a rucksack
containing his other shirt, except I
carried a black cardboard suitcase
and boarded the train, after walking
only two miles: it didn't stop there
unless you raised a flag or,
to be more accurate, fetched from
the waiting room a broomstick
to which a green and grey rag had been
tacked, stood on tiptoe and
shoved it in a rusty iron socket.
The road was muddier
than I had ever seen it
that March day in 1952; I sank
to my ankles, once or twice it
sucked off my shoe.
An old woman emptying slops
called after me, said that she'd pray for me.
Her name was Lilah.
I patted the head
of a half-wild dog.
The wind smelled of sea-salt and sawdust.
I pause at this point to ask
myself if this matters to anyone,
including its author, and decide
at last that it must, if for no other reason
than this: now, nineteen years later,
I sometimes have nightmares in which
it's that same day, but the train

doesn't stop, all the roads are flooded
or blocked with snow, and even
the telephone lines are down,
or, more mysteriously,
the village has been transformed
into an island and there will never be
another boat to the mainland.
When I wake up
the pillow is damp with sweat,
my hands are shaking.

Meeting the Eye of Anybody

POEMS FROM

I'm a Stranger Here Myself
Smoked Glass
I Might Not Tell Everybody This

Stars

I wish I knew the names of all the stars.
But I know only the brightest or nearest, and the others
frighten me sometimes–

not you, old Orion, many-buckled hunter,
nor you, Sirius, cross-eyed hound,
nor you, Aldebaran, bloodshot eye of the bull,

I can pull you down
into the matchbox of my mind;

but I wish I knew
the names of the others.

I would say them aloud now as I walk
alone through the woods and down to the frozen river.

The Palomino Stallion

Though the barn is so warm
that the oats in his manger,
the straw in his bed
seem to give off smoke—

though the wind is so cold,
the snow in the pasture
so deep he'd fall down
and freeze in an hour—

the eleven-month-old
palomino stallion
has gone almost crazy
fighting and pleading
to be let out.

The Road to the Border

Each of us has no choice
but to suffer
for the others.
                    The sacrifice
consists in no more
than bearing one's share
of the pain.
                    I am hitchhiking.
A car stops
fifty yards ahead.
                    I run up to it.
The driver asks me,
"Are you headed for the border?"
And when I tell him, "Yes,"
he says, "So am I," and drives off,
leaving me, revenging himself
on his wife, his kids,
his employer, the government
and God.
                    But if there had been time
and I had been able to
laugh back at him and shout,
"Good luck," instead of
"You bastard," we both might have been
happier now.
                    I know that I would.

In the Shopping Center

Bricks that would melt and drip
if touched by heat, a grate of the same
material, and flames
that burn nothing—a plastic fireplace
seems the perfect symbol
for this shopping center
where almost everything reminds me
of an island touched once,
briefly, long ago
by civilization:
we remember how things looked
but never clearly understood
their purposes, and know nothing
about principles,
so that everything we make
is like the planes the Papuan highlanders
are said to have built
out of wire and cardboard boxes
after the air force left.

The Rites of Manhood

It's snowing hard enough that the taxis aren't running.
I'm walking home, my night's work finished,
long after midnight, with the whole city to myself,
when across the street I see a very young American sailor
standing over a girl who's kneeling on the sidewalk
and refuses to get up although he's yelling at her
to tell him where she lives so he can take her there
before they both freeze. The pair of them are drunk
and my guess is he picked her up in a bar
and later they got separated from his buddies
and at first it was great fun to play at being
an old salt at liberty in a port full of women with
hinges on their heels, but by now he wants only to
find a solution to the infinitely complex
problem of what to do about her before he falls into
the hands of the police or the shore patrol
—and what keeps this from being squalid is
what's happening to him inside:
if there were other sailors here
it would be possible for him
to abandon her where she is and joke about it
later, but he's alone and the guilt can't be
divided into small forgettable pieces;
he's finding out what it means
to be a man and how different it is
from the way that only hours ago he imagined it.

The Jelly Bean Man

"He carries jelly beans," a neighbor told us
when we first came here. "You're lucky you don't
have any small children."
He's the Jelly Bean Man
and the first words he ever said to me
were, "Kiss it and make it well,"
he having observed my wife
bump her forehead against the door
of our car while getting into it
with her arms full of groceries.
"It's nothing to grin about," he said.

So I kissed her above
and between the eyes, and he said,
"Love her; she is the daughter of
Cronos and Rhea, the sister and wife
of Zeus. Here I have a gift for her.
She will share it with you."

And he insisted that she take
two cinnamon rolls
which she and I later ate
at home, very slowly,
with dairy butter
—each bite was like hearing
a little ripple of simple music.

Later we learned it was true
he carried jelly beans and distributed them,
but only as an uncle might or a grandfather
—and, oh, it's so easy to teach
your small daughters and sons
to accept nothing
from strangers, to keep well back always,
to stay out of arm's reach,
to be prepared to run,
so easy to tell them
about evil,
so hard to tell them
about innocence,

so impossible to say:
be good to the Jelly Bean Man
who gives candy to children
from no other motive than love.

Question Period

—While attending a conference
on the teaching of poetry in high schools

I am the victim of cancer called upon to address
an assembly of surgeons. I am the man who built his own house
and did it so well that the architects
drove out from Halifax and questioned him.
"My hands did it," he told them, "and hands don't talk."
I am the farmer who when he was asked why
he had married one woman rather than another said:
"We'd had a good summer followed by a bad winter;
there was a shortage of potatoes in Cuba;
all during January the snow was so deep
I couldn't get to the wood lot;
and she was there."
I am the man who knows The Answerer's
other name is Captain Death.
Blue flowers have appeared
along the edge of the lawn in front of my house,
blue flowers of which I know only
that they are beautiful and don't grow wild
in northeastern North America, and were never planted
by me.
What are they? Where did they come from?
Their secretiveness is like that
of children planning a surprise
for someone they love.
So much whispering.
I will do my best not to hear.

In Praise of the Great Bull Walrus

I wouldn't like to be one
of the walrus people
for the rest of my life
but I wish I could spend
one sunny afternoon
lying on the rocks with them.
I suspect it would be similar
to drinking beer in a tavern
that caters to longshoremen
and won't admit women.
We'd exchange no
cosmic secrets. I'd merely say,
"How yuh doin' you big old walrus?"
and the nearest of
the walrus people
would answer,
"Me? I'm doin' great.
How yuh doin' yourself,
you big old human being, you?"
How good it is to share
the earth with such creatures
and how unthinkable it would have been
to have missed all this
by not being born:
a happy thought, that,
for not being born is
the only tragedy
that we can imagine
but need never fear.

The Night of the Party

Never have I seen women
wiser or more beautiful.

Never have I known men
so witty, so sensitive.

Here in my living room
are the twenty most remarkable
persons in all the world.

And me, the one fool,
who must dance
although too heavy
on his feet, sing
although his vocal cords
are out of tune.

But that is the price
I pay for such
companionship.

My friends,
I do not get drunk for myself,
I get drunk for you.

A Very Common Prescription

I store a tube of tears in my refrigerator.
Many people must do the same.
It has been an excessively dry summer
and you use your eyes more than is good
for them, the doctor said.
At the drug store I was embarrassed
to see what it was
that he had prescribed for me.
Tears! Why, good God, I mean
I cry almost every day of my life.
If I've no better reason
I've only to relax my grip
to have my eyes moisten
at the memory of certain
scenes in old movies:
say, Gregory Peck's funeral
in *The Gunfighter.* Surely,
that ought to be enough.
I was tempted to say this
to the clerk when she handed over
the medication. Lady, it's not
what you think, my heart isn't
made of flint; believe me,
I hurt too. But that wasn't as bad
as reading the fine print
when I got home. Keep tightly
sealed and refrigerate
after use, it said.
If we have house guests I'll hide
the tube at the bottom of
the vegetable crisper.
And to think there are factories!

I picture them as being
windowless, lit by pale blue bulbs,
and containing row upon row
of workers in smocks and hairnets
who sit on long benches, bend
over long tables,
weeping into sterile tissues
for forty hours a week,
men and women who when they're asked
their occupation have to answer:
tear-maker.

Full Circle

In my youth, no one spoke of love
where I lived, except I spoke of it,
and then only in the dark. The word was known
like the name of a city on another continent.
No one called anyone his friend,
although they had friends. Perhaps they were afraid
to commit so much of themselves,
to demand so much of others; for if they'd said,
"We're friends," as they never did,
it would have been a contract.
As it was, they could quarrel,
even hit one another if they were drunk,
and remain friends, never having said it.
Where nothing was sworn there could be no betrayal.
Nor did they touch
casually; their persons seemed to occupy
more space than their bodies did.
Seeing an adult run we'd have looked first for the reason
in the direction from which he came. We never met trains;
my people were like that.
                                        It was not enough for me.
"I love you," I said.
Whispered it, painfully, and was laughed at;
hid until the wounds healed and said it again,
        muttered it.
Wanting to be loved, "I love you," was what I said.
And I learned to touch, as a legless man
learns to walk again.
                                  Came to live among people
who called anyone a friend
who was not an enemy, to whom there were no strangers:

because there were so many, they were invisible.
Now, like everyone else, I send
postcards to acquaintances, With Love—
Love meaning, I suppose, that I remember the recipients
kindly and wish them well. But I say it
less often and will not be surprised
at myself if the time comes when I do not say it,
when I do not touch, except desperately, when I ask
nothing more of others, but greet them with a wink,
as my grandfather might have done, looking up
for an instant from his carpenter's bench.

On the Barrens

"Once when we were hunting cattle
on the barrens,"
so began many of the stories they told,
gathered in the kitchen, a fire still
the focus of life then,
the teapot on the stove as long as
anyone was awake,
mittens and socks left to thaw on
the open oven door,
chunks of pine and birch piled
halfway to the ceiling,
and always a faint smell of smoke
like spice in the air,
the lamps making their peace with
the darkness,
the world not entirely answerable
to man.

They took turns talking, the listeners
puffed their pipes,
he whose turn it was to speak used his
as an instrument,
took his leather pouch from a pocket
of his overalls,
gracefully, rubbed tobacco between
his rough palms
as he set the mood, tamped it into
the bowl
at a moment carefully chosen, scratched
a match when it was
necessary
to prolong the suspense. If his pipe
went out it was no accident,

if he spat in the stove it was done
for a purpose.
When he finished he might lean back
in his chair so that it stood
on two legs; there'd be a short silence.

The barrens were flat clay fields,
twenty miles from the sea
and separated from it by dense woods
and farmlands.
They smelled of salt and the wind
blew there
constantly as it does on the shore
of the North Atlantic.

There had been a time, the older men
said, when someone had owned
the barrens but something had happened
long ago and now anyone who wanted to
could pasture there.
The cattle ran wild all summer,
sinewy little beasts, ginger-colored
with off-white patches,
grazed there on the windswept barrens
and never saw a human
until fall when the men came to round
them up,
sinewy men in rubber boots and tweed caps
with their dogs beside them.

Some of the cattle would by now have
forgotten
there'd been a time before they'd
lived on the barrens.
They'd be truly wild, dangerous, the
men would loose the dogs on them,
mongrel collies, barn dogs with the
dispositions of convicts
who are set over their fellows,
the dogs would go for the nose,
sink their teeth in the tender flesh,
toss the cow on its side,
bleating, hooves flying, but shortly
tractable.
There were a few escaped,
it was said, and in a little while
they were like no other cattle –
the dogs feared them,
they roared at night and the men
lying by their camp-fires
heard them and moaned in their sleep,
the next day tracking them
found where they'd pawed the moss,
where their horns had scraped
bark from the trees – all the stories
agreed
in this: now there was nothing to do
but kill them.

Excerpt from

What Color Is Manitoba?

My family was poor.
Not disadvantaged—curse
that word of the sniffling
middle classes, suggesting
as it does that there's
nothing worse than
not being like them.
We were poor—curse that word, too,
as a stroke victim
half-maddened by his inability
to utter a certain phrase
will say "shit" instead
and be understood.

A sociologist,
belonging by definition to
one of the lesser
of the ruling sub-castes,
comes from Columbia University
to study a community
in Nova Scotia not very different
from where I was born.
A Tutsi witch doctor among Hutus.
He finds, according to
The New York Times, that
almost everyone he meets is crazy.

It's as if a chemist
had analyzed a river
and declared that its water
was an inferior form of fire.

There are secrets I share
with the very old. I know why
we fought in the Boer War
and how in the lumber camps
we cracked the lice between
our thumbnails and it made
a homely sound, was a restful
occupation of an evening:
cracking lice, we were
like women knitting.

Altogether apart
from that, I bear tribal
marks, ritual mutilations.
My brothers and sisters
fill the slums of every
city in North America.
(God knows this is no boast.)
The poor, whom the Russians
used to call the Dark People,
as if it were in the blood.
I know their footsteps.
We meet each other's eyes.

In the Blood

Oh! says my aunt, not
to me but to my all but
stone-deaf uncle,

neither of them
having seen me
since I was a child
and it so awesome
to be together now:

the three of us have
aged thirty years
this afternoon and
they're far from
convinced I'm who
they've been told;
I only half-believe
they're who they say.

Oh! says my aunt, you're
losing your hearing, are
you, that runs in our
family, we all go
deaf as a post,
sooner or later,
didn't anybody
ever tell you?

Nobody ever did.

What's this, says my
uncle, what's this you
say?
        Deaf!
shouts my aunt,
pointing at me.

Did you say deaf, says
my uncle. I nod. My aunt
nods. It has been
established that we bear
the same mark
in our flesh.

We smile, almost
lovingly, at one another.

Curious Encounters

That man coming down
while I go up
the airport escalator
—I know him,

open my mouth to speak
before I realize
it's Johnny Carson.

But what's most
surprising is
his facial expression
is the same as mine was:

the eyes seeming to
stare both
outwards and inwards
as the mind stretches
in both directions,
tries to lift an object
out of the past
into the present and
vice versa—this
in the time it takes
to blink.

The moral being:
nobody gets used to
being known by strangers.

Oh, it's not hard
to get used to crowds,
that's another matter,

but meet the eye
of anybody
with recognition
and for that instant
he'll recognize you.

It's Good to Be Here

I'm in trouble, she said
to him. That was the first
time in history that anyone
had ever spoken of me.

It was 1932 when she
was just fourteen years old
and men like him
worked all day for
one stinking dollar.

There's quinine, she said.
That's bullshit, he told her.

Then she cried and then
for a long time neither of them
said anything at all and then
their voices kept rising until
they were screaming at each other
and then there was another long silence and then
they began to talk very quietly and at last he said,
well, I guess we'll just have to make the best of it.

While I lay curled up,
my heart beating,
in the darkness inside her.

My Beard, Once Lionheart Red

My beard, once Lionheart red, is now yellowish-gray
like a rainy sunset; a child, having seen the statue
in the Victoria and Albert Museum, of Silenus, the satyr
and foster father of Bacchus, and then noticing me
in the crowd, embarrassed her parents by pointing out
the resemblance; and yet, strange to say, I am happier
than when I was a boy and might have passed for the
messenger
from Apollo to Helen, had I worn my hair long, and been
naked, and had I known.

Happier, I suppose because I have all but abandoned
hope of ever reaching
the lost island of answers, of ever catching up
with the tribe
that left me behind as a baby, of meeting my real parents,
the King and Queen, of being adopted officially by God.

Happier, I suppose because I expect less and less
of everybody; where once I wanted all of creation to love me,
I am now almost content to have my presence acknowledged
with a semblance of kindness and a measure of grace.
I rarely make a nuisance of myself, as I so often used to do,
by passing out love, left and right, as if giving away
kittens.

Happier, I suppose because I have tasted enough of fame
to know that it is not flavored with sugar, as I
had thought
when I studied it hungrily in pictures, but with salt;
and, also, that the potion does not transform the one
who drinks it,

but instead creates for him an illusionary twin, in
 whose activities
his part, whether of proud or bemused brother,
is never more than peripheral; people seem to sense this,
for they treat him as if he were not altogether real,
will say to him, casually and with no apparent wish to
 be other than polite,
how amazing it is to find him so fat when he is known
 to be dying, slowly, of cancer.

Happier, I suppose because I was bound hand and foot,
 sewn in a blanket, thrown
into the pool of the man-eating crab, and broke free,
bearing wounds that will tug at me always, like the claws
of beggars, so that I cannot forget how wonderful it is
to get out of bed, stand up and walk, pick up a glass,
fill it with water, lift it to my mouth, and drink, with
 only enough pain
involved in each phase of the process to remind me that
 I am fortune's child, and richly blessed.

What Happened When He Went to the Store for Bread

For Michael Brian Oliver

Because I went to the store for bread
one afternoon when I was eighteen
and arrived there just in time to meet
and be introduced to a man who had stopped
for a bottle of Coca-Cola (I've forgotten his name),
and because this man invited me to visit
a place where I met another man who gave me
the address of yet another man,
this one in another province,
and because I wrote a letter and got an answer
which took me away from the place where I was born,
I am who I am instead of being somebody else.

What would I have been if I hadn't left there
when I did? I would have almost certainly
gone mad; I think I might have killed somebody.
But even if something else had saved me
from madness, I would not be the same person.
I'd have spent thirty years in a different world
and come to look at things in such a different way
that even my memories of childhood and youth
would be different; it might even seem to me now
that there was never anything to escape from.

And then too, there are those who are other
than they would have been, because of some small act
of mine; I played a certain record once
because I liked it, and because he liked it too, a stranger

became my friend and, as such, met the woman
he married, and now they have two children
who would not have been born except for my taste in music.

Carrying the thought farther still, there must be
people in cities that I've never visited
whose lives have changed, perhaps not because of what
I've written but because I wrote: it might be
they didn't like my play and so left early
and because they left early something happened
that would not have happened if they'd stayed–
I put it that way so as not to sound immodest.
God knows, there's not a lot to boast about
when so much seems to depend upon the time of day
a boy goes out to buy a loaf of bread.

The Seasick Sailor, and Others

The awkward young sailor who is always seasick
is the one who will write about ships.
The young man whose soldiering consists in the delivery
of candy and cigarettes to the front
is the one who will write about war.
The man who will never learn to drive a car
and keeps going home to his mother
is the one who will write about the road.

Stranger still, hardly anyone else will write so well
about the sea or war or the road. And then there is the
woman
who has scarcely spoken to a man except her brother
and who works in a room no larger than a closet,
she will write as well as anyone who ever lived
about vast, open spaces and the desires of the flesh;
and that other woman who will live with her sister
and rarely leave her village, she will excel
in portraying men and women in society;
and that woman, in some ways the most wonderful of them all,
who is afraid to go outdoors, who hides when someone knocks,
she will write great poems about the universe inside her.

A Night in 1938, and the Night After

The first time I saw electric
light, the Queen of Heaven
appeared. This was not light
to see by, this was
light to marvel at. All
evening we sat, adults
as well as children, in that
light and did nothing
else. Next day we waited
for Uncle, as head of the
family, to decide the time
had come to switch it on
again. I held my breath
as he pulled the chain, but
the Queen of Heaven did not
return. In a little while,
the adults picked up
the playing cards. Oh!
how I despised them
for that. Then I saw
that the shadows were
gone, the places where
I could roll myself into
a ball or kneel or stand very
still, and not be seen.
I used to do that
and listen. Sometimes, I would
slip out of the shadows when

nobody was looking and
switch cards on them. It was hard
to keep from laughing then.
Now, no matter how
small, quick or quiet
I was, I would never
again have that power.
I could never again
make myself invisible.

Why are you crying?
Uncle asked me.

The Practice of Mercy

Beginning the practice of mercy,
study first to forgive
those who have wronged you.

Having done that,
you will be ready
for the sterner discipline:

learning to forgive those
you have betrayed and cheated.

There Is a Horrible Wing to the Hotel

There is a horrible wing to the hotel.
Unspeakable things happen there.

The toilets are plugged.
There is excrement on the floors
and urine in the bathtubs.

In one room I saw a dog
eating a kitten.

And people live there.
Like that young man with muscular arms
who mistook me for a thief
and would have beaten me with a club
except that I refused to fight back,
knowing that he was so much stronger
that it would be no use.

We became friends, he and I,
and there was a boy who stole
two small triangular pieces
of copper or bronze
from the young man's room
and gave them to me–
I think they may once have been
attached to a trophy.

I hid them when the young man came looking
for them, because I was afraid
of being beaten, and watched him beat the boy.

But one night on the roof we released balloons
in the shape of little animals;
there was a bear, for instance, and a giraffe
which was bright red, and a blue rhinoceros.

They flew very high, those balloons,
and I am afraid of heights, yet I watched them
like everybody else, until they vanished
into that enormous, spinning funnel of blackness.

They flew very high and fast,
and I have never seen anything that looked so free.

Star Light, Star Bright

46 years old—and I still wish
on the evening star.

If I'm alone I even recite the rhyme
under my breath
as I did when I was five.
I've never told this before.
I'm telling you because
you're like me: silly
and afraid of the dark.

Bend closer.
I know a far greater secret:
everyone else is too.

The War Lost

The war lost, the city reduced
to rubble, the long siege
in its final days—
history tells us
that the workers go on
with their work,
as best they can,
clocks are punched,
milk and newspapers
continue to be delivered
within blocks of the enemy's
flamethrowers, husbands and wives
bicker or make love,
children are taken
to the zoo, the theaters
remain open, the amazing
machinery of ordinariness
keeps turning, turning.

A White Book Lies Open

A white book lies open
on the Pope's coffin.

A page rises,
stands upright
for a moment,
falls
and is still.

As if the corpse
had stood up
in its white burial
garments
to draw just one
more breath.

Seeing this,
our ancestors
would have dropped
to their knees.

We call it the wind.

Only When My Heart Freezes

Only when my heart freezes
do I covet the power
to hurt an enemy
as you and I can hurt
each other, my son:
with a thoughtless word,
a careless glance,
an unexpected departure.

You crush your tears
in your fists.
Every door in the house
bangs shut.

And I too am afflicted
like the refugee orphan
who leaves a full table
with breadcrusts
to hide in her pillow.

We understand why
Johnson gave
that terrible shout
when Boswell left him,
without a word,
and galloped ahead
to search out an inn.

"If you had not come back,
I had never spoken to you again,"
the old man said.

The pair of them,
half-mad,
like you and me,
and night falling
in a strange, wild country.

Subway Psalm

It's the first storm of the winter
and the worst since 1888,
the girl on television said.

I keep slipping in my leather-soled shoes.
Twice I've turned into a windmill
in my efforts to keep from falling.

At the top of the stairs leading down
to the subway, Johnnie watches me,
not just with his eyes but with his arms and legs.
He'll do his best to save the old man.

That's how I must have looked at him
when he was five or six years old.
Now he's twenty-six, and it seems
we've traded places.
Why are you laughing?
he asks me.
The honest answer is:
Because you look so funny, standing there
like that, my beautiful son,
and because I've loved you
for such a long time and because this
is the finest storm I've ever seen
and everything is exactly as it should be.

Great Things Have Happened

We were talking about the great things
that have happened in our lifetimes;
and I said, "Oh, I suppose the moon landing
was the greatest thing that has happened
in my time." But, of course, we were all lying.
The truth is the moon landing didn't mean
one-tenth as much to me as one night in 1963
when we lived in a three-room flat in what once had been
the mansion of some Victorian merchant prince
(our kitchen had been a clothes closet, I'm sure),
on a street where by now nobody lived
who could afford to live anywhere else.
That night, the three of us, Claudine, Johnnie and me,
woke up at half-past four in the morning
and ate cinnamon toast together.

"Is that all?" I hear somebody ask.

Oh, but we were silly with sleepiness
and, under our windows, the street-cleaners
were working their machines and conversing in Italian, and
everything was strange without being threatening,
even the tea-kettle whistled differently
than in the daytime: it was like the feeling
you get sometimes in a country you've never visited
before, when the bread doesn't taste quite the same,
the butter is a small adventure, and they put
paprika on the table instead of pepper,
except that there was nobody in this country
except the three of us, half-tipsy with the wonder
of being alive, and wholly enveloped in love.

The Perfectibility of Man

The perfectibility of man—he kept coming back to it,
although it was far from being the only subject that
obsessed him.
He would talk for hours about an imaginary village,
the inhabitants
of which had no need for money, since they grew their
own food
and made everything else—clothes, furniture,
musical instruments—
with their own hands. They would treat their ailments
with herbs.
"We must go back to the soil," he said.
A God-seeker all his life, he read from the
Bhagavad-Gita
every night before he switched off his bed-lamp. He
believed
that children ought to be taught to love animals,
not to hunt them.
But, as has been said, he kept coming back to
the perfectibility of man. "It's a matter of
cleanliness," he said.
"We must begin by delousing the race, though God knows
it's not a pleasant task."
Once, at Posen in 1943, he added this, "I'm not a
heartless beast.
I know, as you do, that it is hellish work we are doing.
I wish to God that I had been spared this task—the horror
of it
burns in my bowels; I am in constant pain. Let us pray that
our descendants
are never required to perform such duties," and in the
presence of the officers
of the Death's Head Division of the S.S., Reichsführer
Himmler wept.

The Thief

Having myself been scared silly when I was young
of any girl made of flesh and, God help us, blood,
I am in sympathy with the boy, said to be slow but not retarded,
who has been taken into custody for stealing panties
from the laundry rooms in our apartment building.
They say he had a trunkful of them. It reminds me
of those other thieves, treated as praiseworthy,
in the old folk tales; Jack of Jack and the Beanstalk
climbing in through a window of a castle to snitch a harp;
it was no crime to rob a giant in those days.
If the King heard about it, he gave the thief his daughter
in marriage; and, as everybody knows that carried with it a guarantee
of living happily ever after. Mind you, that was well before
the invention of panties; for that matter, drawers of any kind
are believed to have been unknown before the 16th century
and, naturally, are first mentioned in a sermon
by the Cardinal-Archbishop of Milan in which he said that God Almighty
intended woman to keep her bottom bare, in remembrance
of Mother Eve's weakness. All that was long, long ago,
and once upon a time; but I can tell you this from experience:
that to a boy like that—who would even today trade his cow, if he had one,

for a handful of beans, not so much because he was
a fool
as because he was too bashful to argue, and
afterwards
hate himself with an almost murderous hatred for being
such a bumpkin–
to a boy like that, every female, without exception,
is a giantess, ready and able to grind his bones to
bake her bread.

How Beautiful Art Thy Feet With Shoes

I suppose it's because so many
poets and artists have never had enough
love from women–as boys they were hideous
in their own eyes, as I was, who thought myself
half-brother to Quasimodo
and looked upon every girl as Esmeralda–
I suppose it's because of this
that they've devoted so much time
to portraying the wonders
of her nakedness, to celebrating
her thighs and breasts
so that some love poems sound more like
commercials for fried chicken,
and hardly ever mention
moments like this when I look up and see you,
through the window, getting out of a cab
with your arms full of Christmas parcels
(they always seem to be
Christmas parcels, even in July and even if
they're only books from the public library)
there must have been times, many times,
over the years, when you came home from somewhere
without your arms filled with parcels,
but I don't remember any of them now,
nor do I recall a time when you didn't come in
either bursting to show me something
or trying to hide something from me:

I've never known anybody so fond of arranging
surprises or so inept at keeping secrets;
and I know how long it takes you to complete
the smallest transaction, how much you like to
look at things and touch them, and how you're always
getting involved in long conversations with
old men in waiting rooms, little kids on tricycles,
the high school students who work part-time in
supermarkets,
how you even say, "Hello, dog," if you meet one–
all this, and so much more, goes through my head
as I catch a glimpse of you, getting out of a cab
with your arms full of parcels, as they always are,
and am reminded suddenly of how much I love you.

Bobby Sands

For Robert Weaver

I did not cry for Bobby Sands, but I almost did,
thinking of my grandmother whom I loved, and who loved me,
and of how her voice would break when she told me again
how her grandmother died in a field in County Wexford
with green stains on her lips, her hands filled with grass,
and of how in that same year the English wagons
escorted by English troops carried Irish grain
down to English vessels for shipment to England. Yes,
yes, that was a long, long time ago; but somebody should
remember Mary Foley, somebody should weep for her,
even if it is only a drunken listener
to lying ballads. Being human, we
each of us can bear no more than a particle
of pain that is not our own; the rest is rhetoric.
Better to shed a tear for Mary Foley
than to rant or babble about suffering
that is beyond our capacity to comprehend.
And what of Bobby Sands? We talk too much,
all of us. In common decency, don't speak
of him unless you have gone at least a day
without food, and be sure you understand
that he loved being alive, the same as you.
Then say what you like. Call him a fool.
Call him a criminal. You'll get no argument
from me. I'll agree with everything
you say in dispraise of gunmen. Oh, but Mary Foley's
ghost was left in my keeping.
I know in my heart that if he had come to me
for a place to hide I could never have shut him out.

He Sits Down on the Floor of a School for the Retarded

I sit down on the floor of a school for the retarded,
a writer of magazine articles accompanying a band
that was met at the door by a child in a man's body
who asked them, "Are you the surprise they promised us?"

It's Ryan's Fancy, Dermot on guitar,
Fergus on banjo, Denis on penny-whistle.
In the eyes of this audience, they're everybody
who has ever appeared on TV. I've been telling lies
to a boy who cried because his favorite detective
hadn't come with us; I said he had sent his love
and no, I didn't think he'd mind if I signed his name
to a scrap of paper: when the boy took it, he said,
"Nobody will ever get this away from me,"
in the voice, more hopeless than defiant,
of one accustomed to finding that his hiding places
have been discovered, used to having objects snatched
out of his hands. Weeks from now I'll send him
another autograph, this one genuine
in the sense of having been signed by somebody
on the same payroll as the star.
Then I'll feel less ashamed. Now everyone is singing,
"Old MacDonald had a farm," and I don't know what to do

about the young woman (I call her a woman
because she's twenty-five at least, but think of her
as a little girl, she plays that part so well,
having known no other), about the young woman who
sits down beside me and, as if it were the most natural
thing in the world, rests her head on my shoulder.

It's nine o'clock in the morning, not an hour for music.
And, at the best of times, I'm uncomfortable
in situations where I'm ignorant
of the accepted etiquette: it's one thing
to jump a fence, quite another thing to blunder
into one in the dark. I look around me
for a teacher to whom to smile out my distress.
They're all busy elsewhere. "Hold me," she whispers. "Hold me."

I put my arm around her. "Hold me tighter."
I do, and she snuggles closer. I half-expect
someone in authority to grab her
or me; I can imagine this being remembered
for ever as the time the sex-crazed writer
publicly fondled the poor retarded girl.
"Hold me," she says again. What does it matter
what anybody thinks? I put my other arm around her,
rest my chin in her hair, thinking of children
real children, and of how they say it, "Hold me,"
and of a patient in a geriatric ward
I once heard crying out to his mother, dead
for half a century, "I'm frightened! Hold me!"
and of a boy-soldier screaming it on the beach
at Dieppe, of Nelson in Hardy's arms,
of Frieda gripping Lawrence's ankle
until he sailed off in his Ship of Death.

It's what we all want, in the end,
to be held, merely to be held,
to be kissed (not necessarily with the lips,
for every touching is a kind of kiss).

Yes, it's what we all want, in the end,
not to be worshipped, not to be admired,
not to be famous, not to be feared,
not even to be loved, but simply to be held.

She hugs me now, this retarded woman, and I hug her.
We are brother and sister, father and daughter,
mother and son, husband and wife.
We are lovers. We are two human beings
huddled together for a little while by the fire
in the Ice Age, two hundred thousand years ago.

Bibliography

Poetry:
The Rose and the Puritan
A Darkness in the Earth
Wind in a Rocky Country
Under the Ice
The Things Which Are
*Bread, Wine and Salt**
*Playing the Jesus Game**
*The Mysterious Naked Man**
*Between Tears and Laughter**
*I'm a Stranger Here Myself**
*Smoked Glass**
*I Might Not Tell Everybody This**
The Gardens of the Wind
Alden Nowlan: Early Poems
An Exchange of Gifts: Poems Selected and New (Robert Gibbs, editor)*

Fiction:
The Wanton Troopers (novel)
Various Persons Named Kevin O'Brien (novel)*
Miracle at Indian River (stories)*
Will Ye Let the Mummers In? (stories)
Nine Micmac Legends

Nonfiction:
Shaped by This Land (with Tom Forrestall)
Campobello
Double Exposure

Plays (with Walter Learning):
Frankenstein
The Incredible Murder of Cardinal Tosca

Alden Nowlan's books marked with an asterisk may be ordered from Stoddart Publishing Co. Ltd., 34 Lesmill Road, Don Mills, Ontario, Canada M3B 2T6, Telephone (416) 445-3333, Fax (416) 445-5967.

About the Editor

THOMAS R. SMITH was born in Chippewa Falls, Wisconsin and majored in English at the University of Wisconsin-River Falls. He was a founding editor of the journal on men and soul, *Inroads,* and presently works as an editor at Ally Press. A poet, essayist, and editor, he is author of a book of poems, *Keeping the Star* (New Rivers Press, 1988) and editor of *Walking Swiftly: Writings and Images on the Occasion of Robert Bly's 65th Birthday* (Ally Press, 1992). He is currently preparing a new collection of poems, *Horse of Earth,* and lives in Minneapolis with his wife, the artist Krista Spieler. He first encountered the poems of Alden Nowlan while traveling in the Maritime Provinces in 1989.